Invasive Animal Species

Bobbie Kalman

🍄 Crabtree Publishing Company

www.crabtreebooks.com

Big Science Ideas

Created by Bobbie Kalman

For our friends Daryl and Irene Rutt,
who add much fun and laughter to our wonderful town

Author

Bobbie Kalman

Photo research

Bobbie Kalman

Editors

Kathy Middleton

Crystal Sikkens

Design

Bobbie Kalman

Katherine Berti

Print and production coordinator

Katherine Berti

Photographs

Ivan_Sabo/Shutterstock: page 31
 (top right)
Lauren Kinsey/sweetmagnoliaphoto.com:
 page 7 (bottom right)
Thinkstock: page 19 (bottom)
Other images by Shutterstock

Library and Archives Canada Cataloguing in Publication

Kalman, Bobbie, author
    Invasive animal species / Bobbie Kalman.

(Big science ideas)
Includes index.
Issued in print and electronic formats.
ISBN 978-0-7787-2783-5 (bound).--ISBN 978-0-7787-2821-4 (paperback).--
ISBN 978-1-4271-8097-1 (html)

    1. Introduced animals--Juvenile literature. I. Title. II. Series:
Kalman, Bobbie. Big science ideas.

QL86.K35 2016   j591.6'2   C2015-908708-2
                                              C2015-908709-0

Library of Congress Cataloging-in-Publication Data

Names: Kalman, Bobbie, author.
Title: Invasive animal species / Bobbie Kalman.
Description: New York, New York : Crabtree
 Publishing Company, [2016] | Series: Big science ideas | Includes
 index. | Description based on print version record and CIP data
 provided by publisher; resource not viewed.
Identifiers: LCCN 2016002036 (print) | LCCN 2016001303 (ebook) |
 ISBN 9781427180971 (electronic HTML) | ISBN 9780778727835
 (reinforced library binding : alk. paper) | ISBN 9780778728214 (pbk. :
 alk. paper)
Subjects: LCSH: Introduced animals--Juvenile literature. | Introduced
 organisms--Juvenile literature. | Biological invasions--Juvenile
 literature.
Classification: LCC QL86 (print) | LCC QL86 .K35 2016 (ebook) | DDC
 578.6/2--dc23
LC record available at http://lccn.loc.gov/2016002036

Crabtree Publishing Company

www.crabtreebooks.com   1-800-387-7650

Printed in Canada/022016/IH20151223

**Published in Canada
Crabtree Publishing**

616 Welland Ave.
St. Catharines, Ontario
L2M 5V6

**Published in the United States
Crabtree Publishing**

PMB 59051
350 Fifth Avenue, 59th Floor
New York, New York 10118

**Published in the United Kingdom
Crabtree Publishing**

Maritime House
Basin Road North, Hove
BN41 1WR

**Published in Australia
Crabtree Publishing**

3 Charles Street
Coburg North
VIC 3058

Contents

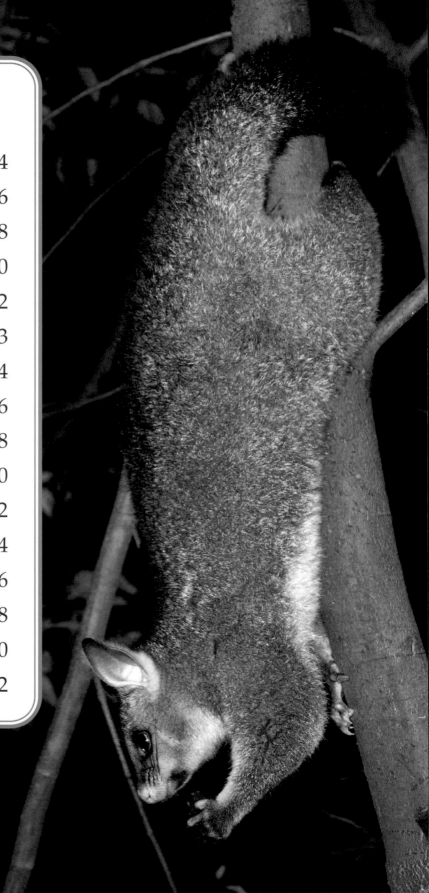

What are invasive species?

Invasive species are plants and animals that do not belong in the **ecosystems** in which they now live. This book is about invasive animals that were taken from one part of the world to live in another. Sometimes these animal "strangers" arrived on ships by accident. Some were introduced by farmers to eat animals or insects that caused damage to crops. Others were brought to new homes as pets. Invasive animals eat the foods that **native** animals need to survive, causing the numbers of some native animals to decrease until they become **endangered**. Endangered animals are in danger of dying out in the **wild**, or places that are not controlled by people.

Find out what problems invasive starlings can cause (see pages 20–21).

Where and why are these cute bunnies invasive? (See page 13.)

Why are red-eared slider turtles not good pets? (See page 23.)

Which invasive animals thrive?

Invasive animals that thrive in new **habitats,** or natural homes, are those that:

- are able to live in many kinds of habitats
- can eat many kinds of plants or animals
- grow quickly and make a lot of babies
- have few **predators** in their new habitat
- can **adapt**, or adjust to, living near humans

*Some people own cats or dogs as pets, but other people like more **exotic** pets that have come from faraway places. Snakes, such as Burmese pythons, red-eared slider turtles, toads, and lizards are bought as pets by people who think they are different and fun. Many of these pet owners soon discover that it is hard to care for these animals and then abandon them in the habitats of native animals.*

Pythons on the loose

The natural home of Burmese pythons is in **marshes**, or grassy **wetlands**, in Southeast Asia. These large snakes eat small animals such as mice, rabbits, and birds. People have captured and brought many pythons to North America to be sold as pets. Most pet owners, however, find these big snakes hard to feed and handle. Thousands of unwanted pet pythons have been abandoned by their owners in Florida's wetlands, known as the Everglades. Pythons have no natural predators there to keep their population down.

Pythons can grow to be more than 20 feet (6 meters) long and weigh 200 pounds (90 kg).

*Pythons are predators that grab their **prey** with their teeth and then squeeze them until they die. These snakes can hurt their owners, especially children! Would this be a good pet for you or this child? Why or why not?*

6

Invading Florida

It is estimated that tens of thousands of pythons now live in the Everglades. These snakes eat many of the same animals eaten by predators native to the Everglades, such as foxes, bobcats, and panthers. This invasive species is causing a decrease in the numbers of prey animals. Some native animals may become endangered because there is not enough prey animals left for them to eat.

Predators such as bobcats and these endangered Florida panthers are losing much of their food to pythons.

Nile monitor lizards

Like the Burmese python, the Nile monitor lizard has become a serious threat to native animals in Florida. These large lizards were brought from southern and central Africa and can grow to be seven feet (2.1 m) long. Sold as pets, many have been released by their owners into the wetlands of Florida where they like to swim and **bask**, or lie in the sun. They have sharp teeth and bad tempers! A Nile monitor's bite has **venom**, which can cause serious pain and illness.

This pet monitor lizard is resting on its owner's feet. Why do you think pet owners might decide that they no longer want to care for a fully grown Nile monitor lizard?

Any food will do!

Monitors eat insects, fish, snakes, turtles, burrowing owls, and many other animals. They especially love the eggs and babies of birds, turtles, and alligators. They are not picky eaters and will also eat dead animals. Because they are so large, these lizards have few predators. Luckily, one of them is the python! Monitors have been seen in swimming pools and on lawns in Florida, causing some people to move from their homes.

Burrowing owls in Florida may become endangered because monitor lizards are eating their eggs and chicks.

Wild pigs

Native to Europe and Asia, wild pigs, also known as wild boars, wild hogs, and feral pigs, were brought to Florida by Spanish explorer Hernando de Soto in the 1500s so people could hunt them. The pigs had many piglets, and soon there were millions of these invasive animals. Today, Texas, Florida, Hawaii, and California have the most wild pigs in the United States. These invasive pigs were also introduced to western Canada in the 1980s as **livestock**, or farm animals, but many of them escaped. Wild boars are social animals that live in large groups and have many piglets. Their piglets, shown below, have stripes along their backs.

piglets

Pig damage!

Wild pigs are **omnivores**, eating both plants and animals. They eat crops and cause damage to native plants by **rooting**, or digging deeply, for food with their big snouts. Rooting disturbs the soil and makes it hard for new plants to grow. When there are not enough wild plants to eat, native animals can starve. By destroying the soil, these pigs cause damage to both the environment and to **food chains**.

bristles

tusks

adult boar

Both male and female boars have tusks that never stop growing. The tusks allow the boars to dig as well as defend themselves. Their main predators are wolves and people. Wild boars can carry dangerous diseases that can be passed on to other animals, such as farm pigs. People can also get sick by eating the meat of diseased livestock.

11

Gray or red?

gray squirrel

red squirrel

Gray squirrels are native to eastern and central North America, but in Britain, Italy, and other European countries, these animals are invasive species! Gray squirrels were introduced to Europe in the 1900s to add variety to local wildlife. At the time, Europe only had red squirrels. Gray squirrels carry a disease called squirrel pox, which can kill red squirrels. They also eat more than red squirrels do, and can store more fat for the winter, so their chances of survival are much better. Europeans love their native red squirrels, but there are now much fewer of these animals.

What do you think?

In Britain, people eat gray squirrels to help get rid of them. Would you eat an invasive animal? (See page 28.)

Trouble with rabbits

In Australia, invasive animals brought from Britain have caused huge problems. In 1859, 24 wild rabbits were taken to Australia and released into the wild for sport hunting. Those few rabbits multiplied into billions because rabbits make babies quickly. Rabbits eat a lot of wild plants as well as farm crops. They feed on **seedlings**, or very young plants, preventing them from growing and making new plants. Rabbits also hurt native animals, such as bilbies, by eating the plants that these animals need to survive.

The program to reduce the number of rabbits in Australia includes destroying their underground dens and introducing viruses that kill rabbits.

Bilbies are a threatened species because rabbits eat their food and red foxes hunt them (see page 14).

Red foxes in Australia

Red foxes were brought to Australia by British settlers so they could take part in the sport of fox hunting, as they did when they lived in England. There are now more than six million of these invasive animals living in Australia. Many animals native only to Australia, such as numbats, bilbies, wallabies, and quokkas, are hunted by red foxes, causing them to become endangered. Foxes not only hunt, they are omnivores that also eat plants. Omnivores are the best survivors because they can find food in many habitats. Which other invasive animals are omnivores?

This quokka mother and her **joey**, or baby, must be very careful to avoid foxes. Foxes have hunted many of these animals.

Numbats are endangered because rabbits eat their food, and foxes eat them. They now live only in a small area in western Australia.

Brush-tailed rock wallabies are decreasing in numbers because red foxes hunt them.

Why not hunt rabbits?

Why are foxes not hunting the invasive rabbits in Australia? Foxes hunt at night while rabbits sleep. Almost every invasive animal is the result of people not learning enough about the animals they are taking from one place to another. What big mistakes have people made that have caused invasive animals to be such a huge problem around the world?

Possums and stoats

Possums were brought to New Zealand from Australia for their fur. Before long, however, people were no longer buying the fur, so the hunting stopped. With no predators in New Zealand, the possums multiplied. Now, millions of these invasive animals are competing with native animals for food such as insects and berries. Possums are also disturbing nesting birds and eating their eggs and chicks.

The kea is a native parrot whose eggs are eaten by possums.

Possums eat trees to death. They do a lot of damage to forests!

Weasels called stoats

Stoats, also known as ermines and weasels, were introduced in New Zealand by Europeans. They hoped that these animals would eat the rabbits taken there, as well as to Australia. Instead of eating rabbits, however, these weasels have eaten many kiwis, New Zealand's national bird. Stoats eat both the eggs and babies of birds. Birds such as the bush wren and laughing owl may have become **extinct**, or have died out, because stoats hunted them.

Kiwis lay huge eggs, which stoats love to eat.

Stoats are a threat to native birds such as kiwis.

Rats and mongooses

Rats can be found all over the world, except in Antarctica. Originally, brown rats came from northern China, but people thought they came from Norway, so the rats are also known as Norway rats. The rats hid on ships sailing from Asia to Europe. Today, brown rats live in cities, suburbs, and farming areas. They live in people's homes, restaurants, and sewer systems. Rats are considered pests, but some rats are pets.

Some brown rats hid in sacks of grain on ships sailing from Asia and Europe to North America. The sacks of grain kept this rat well fed!

Mongooses in Hawaii

Small Asian mongooses were taken from eastern Asia and introduced to Hawaii and most of the Caribbean Islands to control the rats that were eating the sugar crops of farmers. The plan did not work because rats are active at night, whereas mongooses are active during the day. The mongooses did eat some rats, but they also started eating the eggs and babies of Hawaiian birds, such as the nene. Very few of these birds are left.

nene

The mongoose hunts and eats birds, small mammals, reptiles, and insects. It also eats fruits and plants. Birds, such as the nene, and sea turtles, such as the hawksbill sea turtle, are especially at risk. Mongooses eat the eggs and babies of both these endangered animals.

19

Clouds of starlings

European starlings are native to Europe and northwestern Asia but can now be found in North America and most other continents. They live in forests, farmlands, and cities. These hungry omnivores feed on insects, earthworms, and spiders, as well as seeds, plants, and fruits. They are fierce competitors that attack native birds in their nests and destroy their eggs, often driving the birds out of their habitats. European starlings also pose health risks to humans. They carry diseases, and flocks have caused fatal airplane crashes by flying into the engines of planes.

Starlings gather in large groups that can number in the thousands. A large flock can destroy fields of crops. They are also very noisy birds that can imitate the sounds made by other birds, as well as human voices and machine noises.

20

A man named Eugene Schieffelin brought 100 starlings to New York. He wanted to introduce the birds mentioned in the plays of William Shakespeare to Americans. William Shakespeare was a famous British author. The birds he released soon spread all over North and Central America. There are now more than 150 million starlings in these places.

William Shakespeare

Toads and turtles

Native to South and Central America, the cane toad was introduced to Australia to eat the beetles in the sugarcane fields. Unfortunately, they failed to eat the beetles that lived on the upper parts of the cane plants because the toads could not jump high enough to reach them.

More than a billion!

Only 102 cane toads were brought to Australia in 1935, but there are now over 1.5 billion! Female cane toads can lay from 20 to 40 thousand eggs twice a year, so they multiply very quickly! Cane toads have no natural predators because they secrete poisons that kill the animals that eat them. They not only eat the foods of Australian frogs, they also eat the frogs.

Cane toads weigh up to 4 pounds (1.8 kg) and grow to 9 inches (23 cm). They travel quickly on land and in water and eat everything in their path.

poison gland

The poison of the cane toad kills off many predators, even crocodiles. Pets that eat the toads also die.

Red-eared slider turtles

Red-eared slider turtles are native to the southern United States and Mexico, but they are an invasive species in northern places. Sold as pets in the 1940s, 50s, and 60s, this species spread after pet owners released them into local waterways. These turtles are usually very small when they are sold, but they quickly grow large and can live 20 to 40 years. Turtles as pets became popular again in the 1980s with the release of *Tales of the Teenage Mutant Ninja Turtles* books and movies.

Sliders compete with native turtles for food, nesting sites, and places to bask in the sun. They can also pass dangerous diseases to other turtles and humans.

Invasion by water

Oceans, lakes, and rivers are all water habitats that carry animal invaders. Some invaders hitchhike on ships, and others are carried by people as pets. However they move from place to place, invasive water animals change ecosystems, food webs, and people's lives. Three of the biggest invaders are zebra mussels, Asian carp, and lionfish.

Zebra mussels are small freshwater mussels that have stripes like those of zebras. They are native to lakes and rivers in southern Russia but quickly spread to many European countries. They have also invaded the Great Lakes and many rivers in Canada and the United States, traveling to North America on ships. The mussels cling to hard surfaces such as docks and pipes. They clog pipelines in water-treatment plants. The damage these mussels do costs billions of dollars.

Lionfish, native to the waters off Southeast Asia, are believed to have arrived in North America as pets for aquariums. Over time, some were released into the wild. Ocean currents soon carried the fish up the east coast. These fish have no predators because of their sharp fin rays. They eat many kinds of fish, leaving little food for other ocean predators.

fin rays

Asian carp were brought from Asia to North America in the 1960s and 70s to control algae. Since then, they have **migrated**, or moved long distances, through rivers toward the Great Lakes. They are dangerous invaders because they eat the food needed by native fish. They are also dangerous to people. These large carp leap out of the water and can seriously injure people traveling in boats.

City invaders

This baby opossum finds food to eat in someone's back yard.

Even if people did not bring some invasive animals to their new homes, it is still their actions that have caused many animals to move from their native habitats. As cities grow bigger and take up more land, animals that lose their natural habitats move into the cities to find food. Some kinds of animals adapt easily to living near humans, but wild animals in cities often cause big problems for people and their pets.

Skunks are everywhere! If you smell one, it is not far from you. This one is in a city park with people sitting nearby.

City omnivores

Like most invasive animals, omnivores that live in cities have the best chance of survival. Skunks, raccoons, squirrels, foxes, opossums, chipmunks, and many kinds of birds are omnivores. Most are also **scavengers**. Scavengers eat any kind of food they find, including dead animals and garbage.

These baby raccoons are happy about the food someone left outside their door. What problems might people have when they leave food where wild animals can find it?

These coyote pups live in a dead log in a city park. They look cute, but they are predators. Coyotes have killed pet dogs in parks and back yards. They have also attacked people.

Keep wild animals in the wild!

- Do not feed pets outdoors or near your home. Food attracts wild animals.
- Do not set out food for wild animals.
- Pick up fallen fruit around your home.

Eating the enemy

Some people have decided that one way to get rid of animal pests is to eat them. For example, people who have Asian carp in their rivers want them gone because they destroy native fish populations and damage the environment. In Europe, carp is considered a special dish that many people eat on Christmas Eve. In the United States, carp is also showing up in fish markets. Another fish that people in North America are starting to eat is the lionfish. Like salmon, lionfish is high in healthy fats and low in fats that are bad for people.

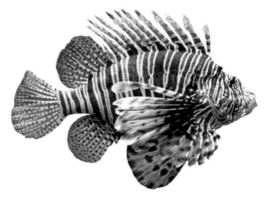

The fin rays of the lionfish contain venom, but its meat does not. It is healthy and delicious. Some restaurants now serve lionfish.

Some people find that carp has too many bones and does not taste great, but many people in Europe love it. Would you try it?

28

Invasive plant foods

Not all invasive species are animals. There are many invasive plants, as well, and some are really good to eat. Look at the foods on these pages. Which ones have you eaten? Which would you like to try?

Wild Himalayan blackberries are found in the Pacific Northwest. The plants grow in thick bushes that block the sun from reaching other plants. These blackberries are good to eat and can be used to make delicious pies and jam.

Watercress, another invasive plant, makes sandwiches look and taste fresh. It is a healthy food that helps fight diseases like cancer.

fennel

Fennel is another invasive plant that can be eaten both raw and cooked. It tastes like licorice. This girl is eating it raw. She likes the taste.

What do you think?

Invasive animals were taken from one part of the world to another for different reasons—from selling the animals as pets to hunting the animals for food, fur, or for sport. The people who took them often did not learn enough about the animals, such as when they slept or were active, or what damage they would do to the ecosystems to which they were introduced. Many took animals to other places to make money. How could people long ago have learned more about animals before taking them to new homes?

How did rats travel to their new homes? Why were mongooses in Hawaii not able to get rid of rats?

How are starlings dangerous to other birds and people? Why were they brought to North America?

Wild boars cause many problems to other animals, people, and the environment. Why were they brought to North America?

Why did British settlers take foxes with them to Australia? Why are they not helpful in getting rid of the invasive rabbits there?

Name five Florida animals that Burmese pythons harm. Why are they not good pets?

How are raccoons invasive even though they are native animals?

The turtles in Teenage Mutant Ninja Turtles *are based on red-eared slider turtles. The release of the book series made these turtles popular again as pets. When owners lost interest in their pets, they let them go in local ponds and swamps. Why is it important to choose pets that you know you will want to keep?*

red-eared slider turtle

Why do people dislike gray squirrels in some places and not mind them in others?

Name three problems caused by invasive rabbits. Which native Australian animal do they harm?

Glossary

Note: Some boldfaced words are defined where they appear in the book

adapt To change to suit a new habitat

bask To lie in the warmth of the sun

ecosystem A community of living things that are connected to one another and to the surroundings in which they live

endangered Describing a plant or animal that is in danger of dying out

extinct Describing a plant or an animal that is no longer found on Earth

food chain A transfer of energy when one animal eats a plant or another animal

habitat The natural place where a plant or animal lives

migrate To travel long distances in search of food or better weather

native A plant, animal, or person whose origins are in a particular area or country

exotic Describing something that is not native and is from a foreign area or country

predator An animal that hunts and eats other animals

prey An animal that is hunted by a predator

venom A poison released by some animals

wetlands Areas of land that are under shallow water some or all of the time

wild Natural places where plants and animals live, which are not controlled by people

Index